Amazon Tap User Guide

Newbie to Expert in 1 Hour!

by Tom Edwards & Jenna Edwards

Other Books By Tom & Jenna Edwards

250+ Best Kindle Fire HDX and HD Apps for the
New Kindle Fire Owner

All New 7" Fire User Guide - Newbie to Expert in 2 Hours!

Amazon Fire HD 6 User Guide - Newbie to Expert in 2 Hours!

Fire HD 8 & 10 User Guide - Newbie to Expert in 2 Hours!

Chromecast User Guide – Newbie to Expert in 1 Hour!

Amazon Fire TV Stick User Guide - Newbie to Expert in 1 Hour!

Amazon Fire TV User Guide - Newbie to Expert in 1 Hour!

Before We Start - Important!

Throughout this book we recommend certain webpages that might be useful to you as an Tap owner and user.

A lot of the webpages we recommend are on Amazon, and a typical Amazon web address might look something like this:

www.amazon.com/dp/B00DBYBNEE?_encoding=UTF8&camp=1789 &creative=9325&linkCode=pf4&linkId=UPTTB3CK67NSPERY&prime CampaignId=prime_assoc_ft

The link above takes you to the Amazon Prime sign-up page, but that's a lot of characters for you to type! So we've used what they call a Link Prettifier to make the links shorter and easier to use.

In this example the shortened link is - www.lyntons.com/USPrime - if you type that into your browser, it will save you lots of typing time, but still take you straight to Amazon Prime....

Contents

Want the Latest Amazon Tap News?

Before we start, we just want to remind you about the **FREE updates** for this book. The Amazon Tap and indeed all media streaming services, like Apple TV, Roku and the Chromecast, are still in their infancy. The landscape is changing all the time with new services, apps and media suppliers appearing daily.

Staying on top of new developments is our job and if you sign up to our free monthly newsletter we will keep you abreast of news, tips and tricks for all your streaming media equipment.

If you want to take advantage of this, sign up for the updates here: www.lyntons.com/updates.

Don't worry; we hate spam as much as you do so we will never share your details with anyone.

INTRODUCTION

Welcome

Welcome and thank you for buying the **Amazon Tap User Guide: Newbie to Expert in 1 Hour!**, a comprehensive introduction and companion guide to the exciting possibilities that the Tap bluetooth speaker and personal assistant has to offer.

Do You Need This Book?

We want to be clear from the very start - if you consider yourself tech savvy, e.g. the kind of electronics user that intuitively knows their way around any new device or is happy Goggling for answers **then you probably don't need this book.**

We are comfortable admitting that you can probably find most of the information in this book somewhere on Amazon's help pages or on the Internet - if, that is, you are willing to spend the time to find it!

And that's the point... this Amazon Tap book is a time saving manual primarily written for those new to streaming media devices, Bluetooth devices and tech that works in tandem with your PC or mobile device.

If you were surprised or dismayed to find how little information comes in the box with your Tap and prefer to have to hand, like so many users, a comprehensive, straightforward, step by step Amazon Tap guide, to finding your way around your new device, **then this book is for you.**

Furthermore the Amazon Tap is a brand new piece of kit and there will be new features, channels and games, not to mention Amazon Tap tips and tricks, appearing constantly over the coming months.

We will be updating this Amazon Tap manual as these developments unfold, making it an invaluable resource for even the tech savvy.

Even if you are buying the first edition of this Amazon Echo instruction book, never fear, you too can keep up to speed with all the new Amazon Echo updates by signing up to our free email newsletter here - www.lyntons.com/updates - so you'll never miss a thing.

How To Use This Book

Feel free to dip in and out of different chapters, but we would suggest reading the whole book from start to finish to get a clear overview of all the information contained. We have purposely kept this book short, sweet and to the point so that you can consume it in an hour and get straight on with enjoying your Amazon Tap.

This Amazon Tap user manual aims to answer any questions you might have and offer Amazon Tap information including,

- What is the Amazon Tap and how does it work?
- What does the Tap do?
- How to setup your Tap
- How to setup Alexa
- How to manage your Amazon Tap account
- Amazon Tap and Alexa
- Amazon Tap tips
- Amazon Tap specifications
- Amazon Tap settings
- And a general Amazon Tap review

This Amazon Tap tutorial will also look closely at Amazon Tap features including:

- The Amazon Tap Alexa app
- Amazon Tap extras
- The Amazon Tap shopping list and to do list
- Amazon Tap radio, music and news
- How to use Amazon Tap IFTTT

- Amazon Tap smart devices (including home hubs and lights)
- Amazon Tap accessories
- Plus much, much more....

And for further Amazon Tap customer support we have links to

- Amazon Tap customer service
- Amazon Tap discussion forums
- Amazon Tap feedback
- Amazon Tap quick start guide
- Amazon Tap videos
- Amazon Tap Help Pages, help desk and community

As we will be updating this book on a regular basis we would love to get your feedback, so if there is a feature that you find confusing or something else that you feel we've missed then please let us know by emailing us at ReachMe@Lyntons.com. Thank you!

So without further ado let's begin.....

1. WHAT IS THE AMAZON TAP?

The Amazon Tap is a sleek personal assistant disguised as a portable Bluetooth speaker that is becoming more useful all the time. Amazon is consistently developing new capabilities and updating your Tap via a Wi-Fi connection. While you might first think that the Amazon Tap is little more than a technological novelty that can do a few cool things, it has become a valued asset in the time we've been using it.

We turn to the Tap throughout the day, for news, weather, music and general information. It assists us in many ways with time management and scheduling, home automation, online purchasing, communication and social media, with more uses being added on a regular basis.

This guide will help you get the most fun and functionality from your Amazon Tap. We want to set your mind at ease from the very beginning: **Setting up the Amazon Tap is very simple**. From there, each step in tailoring this smart device to fit your lifestyle is easy and takes just a few minutes.

Unlike the Amazon Echo there's no "wake word" that you need to use to start voice activation. The Amazon Tap has a microphone button on the front which you "tap" to start your conversation. That said we've already been using the Amazon Echo for the best part of a year now so we're pretty used to using Alexa's name when asking for anything even though you don't need too with the Tap!

With the Tap, just "tap" the microphone button at the top to start speaking. There's no need to hold the microphone button down as you talk and once a conversation has been initiated you won't need to tap the button again, Alexa will already be listening for any replies you need to make.

Talking with the device really is like a conversation due to its pleasant and fluid voice, and "she" will soon be assisting you in lots of wonderful ways.

The Alexa App is a vital piece of the Amazon Tap system. In short, the App is a piece of software easily downloaded to your smart phone, tablet or PC, and it works in tandem with the Tap to allow you to get the most from its capabilities.

The app is, essentially, the remote control center for the Tap. We explain it fully in this guide, see **Chapter 4**.

Voice recognition software is the key to your communication with the Amazon Tap. The device is programmed to understand North American English and will comprehend most users without a problem.

We've had some fun speaking to the device using exaggerated intonations and inflections including a variety of badly performed accents, and Alexa has understood us remarkably well. If you do, however, experience a communication barrier, don't despair. The Amazon Alexa App provides Alexa with voice training. The technology "teaches" the Tap to understand you when you say things like…

- *What time is it?*

- *Set an alarm for 8 a.m.*

- *Set the timer for 10 minutes.*

- *How is traffic?*

- *How many cups in a quart?*

- *Tell me a joke.*

- *Play music by Bruno Mars.*

- *What is the weather in Chicago?*

- *Add olive oil to my shopping list.*

- *Remind me to do the laundry.*

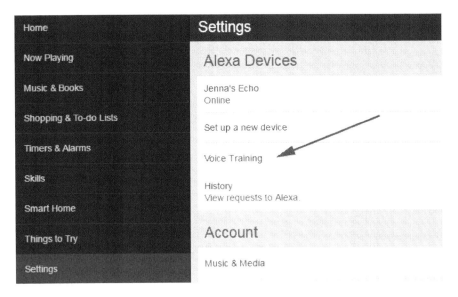

Voice Training can be found within the **Settings** tab is at the bottom of the left side of the app page, and you might have to scroll down to locate it, but more about where to find that later. For now just be reassured that Alexa has smart recognition software that will understand what you say.

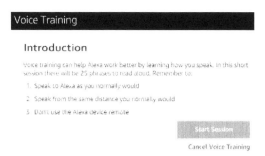

During the Voice Training session, you'll be asked to repeat 25 phrases to give the Tap software the opportunity to "learn" how you speak.

Tap's Technical Specs

Let's have a look at this lithe and lightweight tube of technology. The Amazon Tap is available in black, black or black! However, for an extra $20, you can purchase a rubbery Amazon Tap Sling available at launch in six colors. The Tap Sling has an eyelet ideal for attaching the device to a backpack strap, belt loop or similar using a carabiner clip.

The Tap cylinder is roughly 6.2 inches tall and 2.6 inches wide across the top (159mm x 66mm), or about one-third smaller than the Amazon Echo. It weighs in at 16.6oz (470g), heavy enough to give it a substantial, quality feel but light enough to carry anywhere, especially when clipped on like an accessory.

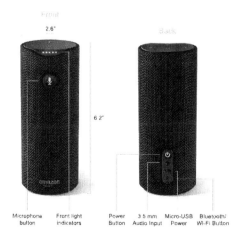

Physical features of this device include the power button on back. The device must first be turned on. The microphone button must then be pressed in order to wake the Tap and start it listening. There's no wake word for the Tap as there is for the Echo, and that's, apparently, how it got its name. According to Amazon, designing the Tap without wake-word functionality saves battery life. It's not constantly using energy to listen for you to call its name.

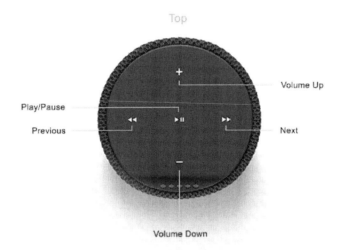

The microphone button is on the side; Amazon saved the limited space on the Tap's top for player functions Play, Pause, Back, Forward and volume Up and Down. There's also a row of 5 LED blue lights that shine when the Tap is listening.

There's one slight issue with the microphone button being on the side rather than the top where you could simply push or tap it when the device was sitting on a flat surface or in its cradle. Instead, you must oppose the "tap" with your fingers if administering it with your thumb, or vice versa. Otherwise, the device would be known as the **Tap it Over, Stand it Back Up**. On the other hand, when the Tap is functioning as a hand-held device, the microphone button placement makes sense.

The internal microphones do a very good job picking up your voice from any side direction and from above. In a noisy environment, you'll want to pick up the Tap and hold it close while you address it. There is currently no remote for the Amazon Tap.

Once again, to talk to Alexa just tap the microphone button and speak, you don't need to hold down the button and indeed there's no need to tap the button again before you speak once a conversation with Alexa has begun.

The Tap's lack of a power cord makes it portable and sets it apart from the Amazon Echo. Its rechargeable battery puts it in a league with competitors like the JBL Flip 3 ($97), Bose Soundlink Color $116) and the UE Boom 2 ($180).

A charging cradle (0.6" x 2.6"/15mm x 66mm and 3.8oz/109g)) with power cord is part of what you get for the $130 price tag. A MicroUSB port gives you another way to charge the device. The Tap nestles easily onto the cradle, and when fully charged, delivers about 9 hours of playback, which we can attest to from experience. On standby, Amazon claims the battery will last up to 3 weeks, a statement we haven't verified. It is hard to imagine anyone letting the Tap sit unused for more than a day or two! It's that handy.

The sound emanating from the Amazon Tap is surprisingly good. It is delivered in 360 degrees by dual 1.5-inch drivers with Dolby sound processing. Dual passive radiators provide bass extension. A 3.5mm audio input in back gives you listening options.

This is a Bluetooth speaker, so playing music stored on other Bluetooth devices through the Tap is a quick and simple process described below. The Bluetooth connectivity includes A2DP for streaming audio and AVRCP for voice control of connected mobile devices.

How Does it Compare With the Competition?

The Tap is a very intelligent personal assistant. As a portable device, it is being compared with Siri, a feature of the iOS mobile operating system in Apple devices including iPhones.

Where the Tap wins: Alexa's voice sounds much more natural than Siri's. The Tap's functionality is greater too, in my opinion. It can simply do more than Siri is designed to do, especially with the growing number of Skills in the Alexa App. The full scope of the Tap's capabilities is explored throughout this book.

Where Siri has an advantage: If you're a creature of habit and a fan of Siri, you'll probably reach for your phone rather than the Tap to request one of the many tasks Siri and the Amazon Tap can both do.

Since the Amazon Tap is also a Bluetooth speaker, comparisons with competitors are in order. Let's put its capabilities head to head with the devices mentioned above: JBL Flip 3 ($97), Bose Soundlink Color $116) and the UE Boom 2 ($180).

- **Battery-powered:** All

- **Bluetooth:** All

- **Stereo sound:** All

- **Dolby:** Only the Tap

- **Voice control:** Only the Tap

- **Wi-Fi music streaming:** Only the Tap (Prime Music, Pandora, Spotify, iHeartRadio, Tunein)

- **Works with mobile hotspots:** Only the Tap

- **Charging cradle:** Only the Tap

- **Personal assistant capabilities:** Only the Tap (Alexa)

2. SETTING UP YOUR AMAZON TAP

The setup was super-quick, and much of it happened automatically with little or no input from us. Here are the details.

What's in the Box

- Amazon Tap

- Charging Cradle

- Micro USB cable and adapter

- Quick Start Guide

Setting up the Main Unit and Accessing the Alexa App

Setting up the Amazon Tap takes just a few minutes using the quick-start guide included in the package, and it worked flawlessly when we tried it.

When setting up for the first time, place your Tap into its charging cradle and plug it into the mains using the micro USB cable and power adapter.

When that's done visit alexa.amazon.com on the device (mobile phone, tablet or pc) that you intend to use for controlling the Tap via the Alexa app.

On a mobile device you will then click Download and will be redirected to the relevant appstore for your device where you can download the Alexa app. Should you for some reason want to do this independently of the setup process you can visit this page - www.lyntons.com/echoapp - to access the following app stores:

- Amazon Appstore

- Google Play

- Apple App Store

The app can also be used on your computer using a supported browser, currently Chrome, Safari, Firefox and Internet Explorer. Again just type in alexa.amazon.com to get started. When using your computer to access and operate the app everything is done in your browser so you won't be downloading any software using this method.

Once you have access to the Alexa app...switch your Tap on at the power button. The 5 led buttons at the top of the Tap should turn blue and the orange and Alexa will say "***Hello***". You are now ready to setup your Tap and connect to Wi-Fi

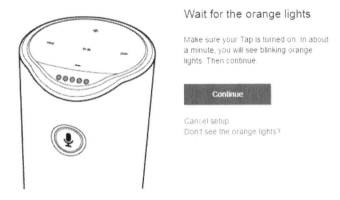

Wait for the orange lights

Make sure your Tap is turned on. In about a minute, you will see blinking orange lights. Then continue.

Continue

Cancel setup
Don't see the orange lights?

Connecting to Wi-Fi

Turn your attention to the Alexa App which will walk you through the short process of connecting the Amazon Tap to a Wi-Fi network. Have your Wi-Fi password available. The password is usually located on the Wi-Fi router. If it's not there, contact the company that provides your Internet service.

Note: the Tap does not support enterprise or ad-hoc/peer-to-peer networks, though it is unlikely that your network is one of these types.

If for some reason the setup process does not start immediately within the Alexa app then follow these instructions which are also the instructions you should follow if and when you connect to different Wi-Fi networks in the future.

Press and hold the Bluetooth/Wi-Fi button towards the bottom of your Tap for 5 seconds to make it discoverable. Then go to the Amazon Alexa App homepage. Open the navigation panel on the left, and select **Settings >Set up a new device>Tap**. By the way, this sequence means you should:

1. Select **Settings** from the options on the Amazon Alexa App homepage

2. Select **Set up a new device** from the options that appear

3. Select **Tap** from the fresh set of options you're given

The 5 LED lights should flash orange.

NB. If you have already setup your Tap once and now want to connect it to a different Wi-Fi network, at step 2 above, rather than selecting **Set up a new device** select **Update Wi-Fi** to join a different network.

In the app, once the orange light appears a list of one or more Wi-Fi networks will appear. Choose your Wi-Fi network, and enter the network password if necessary. Select **Connect**. If your network isn't on the list, scroll down to select **Re-scan** to search again or choose **Add a Network** and follow the instructions that appear.

When we did this, we didn't strictly time the process. It seemed to take more than a minute and less than three for the Tap to connect to the network. When it did connect, a confirmation message appeared on the **Set up a new Tap** page of the app....so be patient.

You're now ready to return to the app Home Page, which you'll find at the top left of the screen, to begin using your Amazon Tap.

Before we move on, now is probably a good time to look again at the 5 led lights at the top of you tap and decipher what their different colors and indications mean.

- **Pulsing blue light over cyan lights from left to right:** The Echo is starting up when first plugged in.

- **All continuous cyan lights:** You have pressed the microphone button and the Amazon Tap is waiting for you to speak

- **All cyan lights pulsing:** The Tap is replying or responding to your request.

- **Quick pulsing orange lights moving from left to right:** The Amazon Tap is in setup mode.

- **Blue lights pulse on and off:** The Tap is getting ready to pair via Bluetooth

- **Pulsing red lights:** These are error lights indicating the Tap is unable to complete your request.

3. USING THE TAP AS A BLUETOOTH SPEAKER

One of the attractive features of the Amazon Tap is that it can be used as a free-standing Bluetooth speaker, and the sound quality is very good. This enables you to stream music or other content from any Bluetooth-equipped device such as your phone, tablet or computer.

To stream content using the Tap as a Bluetooth speaker, it must first be paired to the device containing the content you want to hear. This is done by finding and accessing the Bluetooth settings of the PC, phone or tablet you want to pair your Tap with.

Obviously the location of the Bluetooth settings will vary from device to device, they are typically found in the general Settings menu of your device. On a computer, they are usually found using the search function. For example, you can use the search box on the Start panel for Windows to find the Bluetooth settings.

By far the simplest way to pair your Tap with another device is to press the **Bluetooth/Wi-Fi** Button at the base of your Tap for a second to make it discoverable; Alexa will tell you that it is ready to pair. You should then be able to see your Tap displayed within the Bluetooth settings of the PC, phone or tablet you are trying to pair it with. Click on the icon representing your Tap and both devices will pair. Again Alexa will let you know that it has successfully paired to your device.

You can also prepare your Tap for Bluetooth pairing by tapping the microphone button and saying "*Pair*". Personally we always use the Bluetooth/Wi-Fi button.

When a Bluetooth device is paired to your Tap, you can either control the audio you are listening to by using the control buttons on the top of your Tap or you can press the microphone button and use voice commands like,

- *Play*

- *Pause*

- *Previous*

- *Next*

- *Stop*

- *Resume*

- *Restart*

It should be stressed that before you can use these commands you need to start playing something via your paired device, play an album in your iTunes app for example. We found through experience, though the information is on Amazon too, that if while streaming via Bluetooth you start asking Alexa for specific songs, albums or artists from the music stored on your phone or other Bluetooth device, the Tap will disconnect from Bluetooth and start searching for the music in your Amazon Music library or other music service. So you can only use the simple voice commands above to control content that is already playing.

If your Bluetooth connection is disconnected you can reconnect to the Bluetooth device by simply pressing the microphone button and saying "*Connect*", wait for your devices to pair again and press play on the device to continue listening.

If you run into problems pairing to a particular Bluetooth device (you may have multiple devices you regularly pair with) the simplest option is to start afresh. Within the Alexa app go to **Settings** and select your Tap and then select **Bluetooth** and then **Clear**. Now try connecting again to the Bluetooth device of choice and you should be fine.

Finally, if and when you want to disconnect your Tap from Bluetooth pairing just press the power button once.

Unfortunately, the Tap can't yet receive phone calls, text messages or other notifications from your mobile device. Additionally, audio from the Amazon Tap can't be sent to other Bluetooth speakers or headphones.

4. AMAZON ALEXA APP BASICS

The smart Tap Bluetooth speaker and the Amazon Alexa app work together as a team to create a really cool personal assistant that we expect to become more competent as time goes by, via Amazon updates and the addition of new third-party partners. Together, the app and device form a system called Amazon Tap. This chapter is an overview of the Alexa app and how to use it.

We first explored the app on our laptop because navigation is simpler and the large screen is easier to see. Once we were familiar with the app, working with it from a cell phone is a snap.

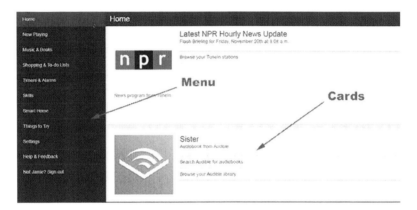

The Home Screen is divided into two sections. The Menu is on the left edge, and the rest of the screen is taken up with the dialog cards. One card is created for each request made of Amazon Tap.

When you select the down arrow on any card, the option is given to provide feedback to improve your Amazon Tap's voice recognition. What Alexa heard is listed with the question, "***Did Alexa hear you correctly?***" Answer ***Yes*** or ***No***. You've also got the option to remove the card.

At first, we gave feedback and deleted a few cards to reduce clutter, but we mostly forgot about it pretty quickly.

Now the only time we choose the down arrow and give feedback is if the Tap did not hear us correctly, a rare occurrence. We also occasionally scroll back through the cards to locate a song/playlist/ station we enjoyed but forgot to get the name of.

Depending on the type of request that produced the card, you'll have more options. For example, if you've requested Tap to play something from your Amazon Music Library, the card includes options to **Search the Amazon Digital Music Store** for similar music, **Search Amazon Prime** for free music and Browse your library for similar choices.

Cards for information requests will include the option to Search Bing for the topic.

If you choose the **Learn More** option in blue on any card or at the top of the list of cards, the Amazon Tap FAQs appear. There are 12 questions, and they're worth reading over.

The Amazon Alexa app menu on the left gives these choices:

- **Home:** When Home is selected, your list of cards appears.

- **Music & Books:** Within this section are the following audio options

  - **Your Music Library:** All your purchased and free music from Amazon is available here.
  - **Prime Music:** If you have an Amazon Prime membership, you can access more than 1 million songs, albums and artists here; if you don't, choosing this tab will take you to an Amazon Prime signup page.
  - **Spotify:** Synch your Spotify account with Amazon Tap, and play your tunes through its Bluetooth speaker.
  - **Pandora:** Synch your Pandora account with Amazon Tap, and play your tunes through its Bluetooth **speaker.**
  - **iHeartRadio & Tunein:** Create accounts with these streaming radio services, and make the most of them with

Amazon Tap.

- **Audible:** If you're an audiobook fan, this is where you make the most of your books using Tap.
- **Kindle Books:** Have Alexa read your Kindle books to you.

- **Shopping & To-do Lists:** For shopping, Add by voice or manually; cross off items you've purchased; shop for the object on Amazon or Bing. For To-do lists add by voice or manually; keep track of what's been done and still needs doing.

- **Timers & Alarms:** Set, pause, continue and cancel timers up to 23:59:59. Set an alarms for up to 24 hours, and toggle it on or off.

- **Skills:** Discover the ever growing list of extra functions and fun developed by third party companies

- **Smart Home:** Set up and manage your smart home devices

- **Things to Try:** This list shows you how to get the most from Amazon Tap through topics like What's new, Do more with your Tap and tips for managing the app.

- **Settings:** We'll refer to Settings throughout this guide to help you manage your Amazon Tap and account.

- **Help & Feedback:** Just what it says - answers to all your questions including the Amazon Tap User Guide.

You can manage the history of your dialog with Amazon Tap in much the same way as you manage your computer's history. Go to *Settings > History* where you'll find the complete list of requests and commands.

We occasionally scroll down the list to find a station we were playing or retrieve an answer to a question we asked. Provide feedback or delete any request by selecting the down arrow.

If you prefer to delete all voice recordings, go to ***Manage your Content and Devices***, and select the ***Your Devices*** tab. Choose the Tap, and a popup window will appear where you can delete or cancel the delete request. Keep in mind that Amazon Tap has been learning how you speak to give more consistently accurate answers. If you delete your voice recordings, you might find that the Tap's ability to understand you is reduced. See our **chapter on Security** for more information.

Now that you've been introduced to your new personal assistant, it's time to get to know Alexa more thoroughly and find out what her true capabilities are.

We've created this section from our experience, and it's intended to be a guide you can refer to in the days ahead to maximize the fun and usefulness of your Amazon Tap and to minimize the hassle. Let's start with the Tap's strongest feature...Audio!

5. MUSIC, RADIO AND BOOKS

We're music fans, and you probably are too. Amazon gets this, so it built the Tap to deliver real listening pleasure. Let's look at the top music and book services supported by the Amazon Tap that can all be found when you click the Music & Books tab in the left sidebar of the Alexa app.

Amazon Prime Music: What it Offers

There's a long list of benefits for using Amazon Prime including Prime Music. There's a 30-day free trial here - www.amazon. com/dp/B00DBYBNEE - if you want to try it out before making a commitment.

With Prime Music, available to Prime members in the U.S. and U.K., you have unlimited ad-free access to more than a million songs in addition to complete albums and stations created for all major music genres.

Within the Amazon Alexa app, there are two Amazon music tabs to choose from. The first tab is *Your Music Library* which contains all songs, albums and lists you have downloaded in your standard Amazon account.

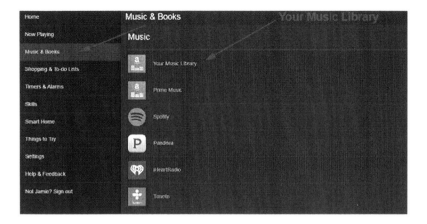

Using the Amazon Music Importer, you can add up to 250 songs from your computer to your Amazon Music Library to play on Amazon Tap and other devices. We explain more about Prime Music and downloading or uploading music to and from your Amazon Music Library in our book **Amazon Prime & Kindle Unlimited Newbie to Expert in 1 Hour!** - www.amazon.com/dp/B00WZY5DVK

The second tab is the Prime Music tab where you can browse all Stations, Genres and Playlists that are available to Prime members.

Setting Up your Prime Music Account

When you order Amazon Prime, you'll be taken to the Prime Welcome page where you can explore its benefits including Prime Music. Scroll down the page to the music information and choose "Discover Prime Music".

In addition to the Tap, you can listen to Prime Music on a wide range of devices including iOS and Android phones, your PC or Mac and Amazon products such as the Fire phone, Fire tablet and Fire TV Stick.

It would be an understatement to say that there are a lot of musical options on the Prime Music homepage. Frankly, there are so many options, and so many of them overlap, that it was initially confusing.

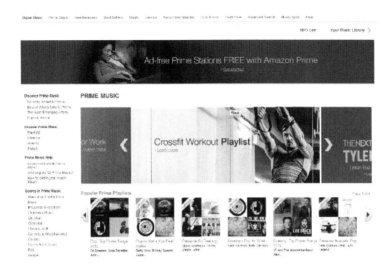

Think of it this way: The Amazon Prime music categories discussed below attempt to organize the entire catalog of modern music into logical groups which Amazon term as Stations, Genres and Playlists. There aren't hard and fast distinctions between these groups.

We quickly realized that there are just too many options to get a handle on easily so we adopted an adventurous, open-minded attitude. We pick a station or playlist that sounds good to us, and wait to hear what songs are included in the collection. We then note the station and return to it or avoid it based on our tastes.

Okay, with that perspective in mind, here is an overview of the musical groupings. Take a relaxed hour or so to explore what's available and get a feel for what directions you want to explore first.

All Stations: The dozens of stations cover all the musical styles we're familiar with, and we're music buffs, plus lots we're not acquainted with but look forward to exploring. Here's something we didn't expect when we began to listen: Stations named for a specific artist play that artist as well as similar artists. For example, the James Taylor station plays plenty of JT, of course, but also Christopher Cross, Joni Mitchell, Jim Croce, Gordon Lightfoot, Carole King, Jackson Browne, etc.

Genres: The genres are divided into favorites such as Alternative, Blues, Children's Music, Classical, Classic Rock, Decades, Gospel and Pop. Each genre offers stations named for artists, decades and styles.

Playlists: There are thousands of Playlists that give you a more specific slice of the types of music you like, and your options are incredibly diverse. You can search Playlists by genre, artist, mood or decade to locate those that appeal to you. Select "***Add Playlist to Library***" and the list will be stored there to be played on your Amazon Tap, phone or other device using the Alexa app.

Albums & Songs: More than 1.5 million songs and almost a thousand complete albums are available for you to add to your Music Library.

See what we mean? Amazon Prime offers a torrent of music, and there are innumerable places to jump into the rushing waters. We think you'll enjoy the ride, as we do.

Controlling Prime Music with your Echo and App

Using voice, it is as easy as saying, "***Play Classical for Focus***" to get the music started. The Amazon Tap will reply with "***The Playlist Classical for Focus***," and Bach's Brandenburg Concerto No. 3, Handel's Water Music Suite No. 1 and other great pieces will fill the air through the Tap's quality speaker. Once the chosen list is playing, Alexa will respond to commands that control the music. These include:

- *What's playing?*

- *Turn it up or Softer*

- *Volume 5*

- *Skip* or *Next Song*

- *Pause, Resume* or *Continue*

- *Loop*

- *Stop*

- *Continue*

- *Buy this song*

- *Add this song* (to your Amazon Music Library)

When using the Alexa app instead of your voice, simple taps or clicks are all that are needed to choose the music you want to play. When you've made your choice, a player appears with options for play, pause, skip ahead, go back or shuffle the music.

You can also select the *Thumbs Up* or *Thumbs Down* symbols, or say, "*I like/dislike that song*". Alexa will respond with, "*Okay, rating saved*", and Prime will remember your preferences for the next time you select that Station or Playlist.

Spotify: What it Offers

This Swedish streaming service hooked up with Alexa after Pandora, iHeartRadio and several others were onboard (see below). In similar fashion, Spotify delivers music (30 million songs and counting) and podcasts to Tap users through searchable artists, albums, labels, genres and playlists.

While Spotify has both Free and Premium subscriptions, you'll need to go with Premium to listen to the service with your Tap. The current cost for Spotify Premium is $9.99, but a 30-day free trial is available that gives you ad-free streaming, unlimited skips and play any track features.

Setting up Your Spotify Account

Once you've established a Spotify account, synching it to the Alexa App on your laptop or phone will take just a couple of minutes.

Open the Alexa App then click on the Music & Books tab on the left hand side and then the Spotify tab. Choose Link Account and then log into Spotify with Facebook or with your username and password. If you don't yet have a Spotify account you can register for a Premium account at this point.

Controlling Spotify with the Alexa App

Using voice commands: Speaking directly to the Tap ask, "*Play Twenty One Pilots on Spotify*." It's important to include "*on Spotify*" or Alexa will typically select music from Amazon Prime or another music service first. You can ask for a specific song name, playlist name, genre, artist, composer or Discover Weekly to hear what's new. For example, say, "***Play songs by Carrie Underwood on Spotify***," or "***Play Work by Rihanna on Spotify***."

Once your music has started playing other voice command options are what you'd expect: "Pause, resume, stop, mute, previous, next, shuffle, skip this song, volume 1-10, volume up/down, etc.."

You can also get answers to questions like, "***what song is playing?***" and "***who is this artist?***"

Using the Alexa App: The Player in the App shows you the current artists and gives you standard command options such as play, pause, skip, previous, next and shuffle.

Using the Spotify App on your phone: Select ***Amazon Tap*** from the device list. From there, voice commands will work.

Unlinking Spotify and Amazon Accounts

If you don't want the accounts linked: Open the Alexa App, browse the Menu, and choose ***Settings***. Choose ***Music & Media*** and choose ***Spotify*** from the list. Choose ***Unlink account from Alexa*** and finally choose the ***Unlink*** option.

Pandora: What it Offers

Pandora offers hundreds of customized stations in more than 40 genres. There are standards such as Blues, Classical and Comedy and quite a few unique offerings like BBQ, Festivals and MusicaRomantica.

Setting Up your Pandora Account

Select the *Music & Books* tab on the left side of the Alexa app and then *Pandora* to get started. You'll have the option of signing in to an existing Pandora account or registering a new one. A new account requires providing your email, user name, password, gender and zip code.

Once you've signed in or created an account, Pandora is immediately supported by Amazon Tap. For those with an existing account, your stations will appear in My Stations, and you can alter or delete them as you wish.

Pandora Basic is free, but short commercials occasionally play between tracks. An upgrade to a premium account is available on the Pandora site. Premium accounts are ad free and allow more song skips. Currently, the upgrade is $4.99 per month or $54.89 annually.

You can use this link to upgrade - www.pandora.com/one

Controlling Pandora with your Tap and Alexa App

If you've created a new Pandora account, start by selecting the +*Create Station* box at the top of the Pandora page on the Alexa app. From there, you can use the box to search for an artist, genre or track, or you can see what's already available in the Browse Genre section.

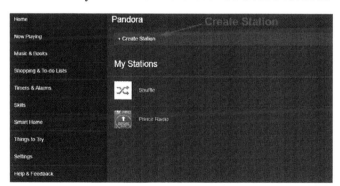

When you select an existing station, it begins to play and also appears in the list entitled My Stations on the Pandora Home Page.

Select the down arrow to have the option of deleting the station. Pandora allows you to create up to 100 of your own stations to supplement what is already available. For example, we're fans of a musical genre called reggaeton, and there's not a pre-existing station for it.

However, when we typed reggaeton into the search box, several tracks came up. We selected the track Reggaeton Latino, and a station was created with that tune and similar songs. We spell this out in detail because there are no "how-to's" given on the app. Some tasks, such as creating our own stations, we learned how to do through trial and error.

However, as far as stations are concerned, there are already so many customizable stations within each genre of music, creating your own might not be something you'll want to do anyway.

Any station's playlist can be customized by eliminating unwanted songs from the list. Do this by saying, "***Thumbs down***", or by selecting the downward-pointing thumb on the player at the bottom of the screen.

Note, however, you'll only be able to delete or skip three songs on any list. The fourth attempt will produce a drop-down menu saying, "Our music licenses limit the number of songs you may skip." In other words, you'll have to listen to the remaining songs all the way through or choose a new station to play.

The Pandora player offers options to play, pause, go forward and go back. If you click or tap the small icon of the album cover for the song playing, you'll get the full page view with a larger icon and a list of the songs as they play.

You'll also have the option here to look at your stations history and the queue of songs that have played on the current station. Choose the down arrow of any of the songs in the queue to rate it, create a song or artist station, shop for the music at the Amazon Digital Store, Bookmark the song or give the song a rest by selecting "I'm tired of this track".

You can use voice commands with Pandora on Tap, just as you can with the other services.

TuneIn: What it Offers

TuneIn is completely free, and setting up an account isn't necessary. However, having an account allows you to "Follow" your favorite stations and shows and to Share them on Facebook, Twitter and Google Plus and Tumblr.

On TuneIn, you've got the opportunity to access more than 100,000 Internet radio stations including FM, AM, HD, LP and digital. Brands featured include ESPN, NPR, Public Radio International, CBS and C-Span. Your browsing options include much more than Music.

There is Local Radio, Sports, News, Talk and By Location along with popular shows featured in all of those genres. There are more than 4 million podcasts, concerts and interviews available too, a fact that sets TuneIn apart from its competitors.

Setting Up your TuneIn Account

As mentioned there's no need to set anything up to use TuneIn, you can access and browse everything on offer by following the instructions below.

However if you do want to take advantage of some further features you can join TuneIn at tunein.com. Signing up is a brief procedure that includes choosing a user name with an associated email address and a password. You also have the option of signing in with an existing Facebook or Google+ account, a step that simplifies accessing a new or existing account.

Once you have an account you can create and organize a library of your preferred categories, songs and artists that can be accessed and played on your Amazon Tap using voice or the app. Similar to Amazon Prime Music, there is a massive amount of content to explore on TuneIn, so enjoy the process of discovery!

Controlling TuneIn with your Echo and App

If you know the radio station name or station call sign or the name of the podcast, you can use voice commands to get exactly what you want. Examples include:

- Play The Bear, 98.1

- Play the Thundering Herd podcast

- Play A Prairie Home Companion

If you simply request the Tap to play NPR or CBS Sports, for example, the appropriate station in your market will be accessed. Ask the Amazon Tap to pause or resume as desired. You can also make other requests (ask a question or add something to your to-do list, e.g.) while TuneIn is playing, and the Tap will reply before returning to TuneIn.

The Alexa app makes using TuneIn a snap. On the left side menu of the app, select Music & Books and then TuneIn and browse with tabs for Local Radio, Trending, Music, Talk, Sports, News, By Location, By Language and Podcasts. Click or tap for dozens of options within each category. When you find what you want, click or tap it, and a player will begin to play the station or show.

IheartRadio: What it Offers

This network is a digital radio and content streaming service that includes thousands of live radio stations and podcasts from the US. iHeartRadio gives you the option to create personalized Custom Stations featuring your favorite artists or genre.

Music is just the beginning. Other categories include Business & Finance, Comedy, Entertainment, Food, Games & Hobbies, Health, News, Politics, Science, Spirituality and Sports. Each group offer numerous and wide-ranging options, so it will take you some time to explore what's available and find shows you want to return to often.

Setting Up your iHeartRadio Account

To enjoy iHeartRadio on your Amazon Tap, no account is necessary. Simply use the Alexa app to explore and listen. However, with an account, you can create Custom Stations and share them with others. Select the iHeartRadio on the Amazon Alexa app and then click "Link your account now" to be taken to a special sign in/sign up page for activating you iHeartRadio with your Tap.

If you don't have an account, set one up using an email address and password. You'll also be asked to provide zip code, gender and agreement with the site's Terms of Service. Another option is to link an existing Facebook or Google Plus account to create an iHeartRadio account.

Controlling iHeartRadio with your Tap and Alexa App

When you click or tap the iHeartRadio tab, from within Music & Books, your options appear in the main screen. They include Search for artist or station, Browse for Favorites you've chosen while using the network.

The Browse option gives choices for Live Radio, Perfect For (Kids, Working Out, Driving and more), iHeartRadio Originals and Shows. We had a lot of fun exploring the variety of choices available.

The Originals tab features dozens of unique stations including Golden Era musical numbers, Sippy Cup for pre-schoolers, Classical Genius featuring Mozart and his contemporaries, Workout Beats, All 60s, Road Trip and Chillax.

To use voice commands to play iHeartRadio, you have to know the name of the show, station or radio program you want to listen to. When requesting a radio station, your best bet to get it working is to refer to it with the exact title of the station as it is shown in the Amazon Alexa app.

Some use call letters; others use a name such as The Bear or Kat Country. We had to experiment in order to access some stations. For example, we requested the station listed as New Country 96.3 KSCS.

When we asked for it by "New Country," the Tap retrieved a top country hits station from Amazon Prime Music. We then asked for KSCS 96.3, and the radio station was properly accessed.

You can make requests of the Tap without first pausing iHeartRadio. The Amazon Tap will respond and then return to playing your iHeartRadio selection. Other control options include "stop, pause, resume, continue, play." As you can see, the device responds to multiple commands for the same function.

For more voice command options for Pandora, IHeartRadio, TuneIn and Prime Stations visit this page on Amazon - www.lyntons.com/voice-command

iTunes on The Amazon Tap

The popular music services iTunes does not have native support on Amazon Tap. In other words, it doesn't integrate with your iTunes account in the same way as it does with the services we've already discussed.

However, if you have an iTunes account or use the iTunes app, you can still play music from iTunes using the Tap. Remember, the Tap is a Bluetooth speaker, so you can pair other devices like your phone, tablet or pc to the speaker and stream your iTunes music that way. The only difference is you will control your music selection with your iTunes software rather than with the Alexa app.

New to Itunes? Then follow this links for more info.

iTunes - www.apple.com/itunes

To pair a mobile device you can either pair using the instruction given in **Chapter 3** (Using the Tap as a Bluetooth Speaker) or, if you wish, you can use the Alexa app, within the app select the **Settings** tab on the left and then your Tap and then the **Bluetooth** option. Choose **Pairing Mode**, and you'll be given the command to locate the Bluetooth settings on the device you wish to pair with the Amazon Tap and to enter the code the Tap provides

So now go to the device you want to pair and open the Bluetooth settings there to finish the connection. That's all you need to do.

Once the device is paired, you'll choose the music that you want to play in iTunes but you will still be able to use voice commands like *"Play, Pause, Stop, Cancel, Resume, Continue"* with your Tap.

Audible: What it Offers

Audible is an Amazon company that creates audiobooks. A standard free 30-day trial includes two free books. If you're an Amazon Prime member, the free trial is 90 days, and you receive three free books during that time. The cost of Audible after the trial period is $14.95 per month and includes one audiobook. Additional books are available in all genres and at a wide range of prices.

Follow this link for more info - www.audible.com

Setting Up your Audible Account

Choose the Music & Books tab on the left side of the page and then Audible from the options shown. It will take you to an Amazon.com page where you can sign into an existing account or establish a new account through a free trial.

If you already have an Amazon.com account, you simply sign into it and start the free trial with a couple of quick steps. If you don't have an Amazon account, starting one is as easy as providing an email and password and a few other details.

Once you've established a free-trial account on Audible, your first credit will appear on the Audible page. Browse the audiobooks and select your choice. You'll have the option of paying for it with the credit or saving your credit and using one of the forms of payment you have stored on Amazon.

Controlling Audible with your Tap and Alexa App

When using the app, choose the Audible tab, and your audiobooks will appear. Select the one you want, and it will begin to play. When you pause the book to use Amazon Tap to listen to music, for example, your place in the book will be marked. When you return to the book, the audio will pick up a few seconds prior to where it left off.

Using voice recognition, give these or similar command:

- *Play Audible book 'The Magic of Thinking Big'*

- *Pause the book*

- *Resume my book*

- *Go forward*

Kindle Books on the Amazon Tap

Even if you don't have an Audible account you can still listen to Alexa reading many of your Kindle books back to you via the Amazon Tap thanks to Alexa's text to speech technology. Kindle ebooks books that you have bought from Amazon's Kindle ebook store or borrowed from the Kindle Owners Lending library will be listed with the Alexa app, if Alexa is able to read it. Just click on the Music & Books tab in the left sidebar of the Alexa App and then Kindle Books to view existing purchases.

Controlling Kindle Books with your Tap and Alexa App

From within the Alexa app, having clicked the Kindle Books tab, you can click on any title to commence playback. A control strip for that book will appear at the bottom of your list of books where you can play or pause the playback, adjust volume and fastforward or rewind in 30 second intervals.

Click on this control strip again and you will be able to select individual chapters from within the book.

Using voice commands with your Tap should be familiar to you now. You can tap the microphone button and use voice commands like,

- *Read* [Kindle book title]

- *Skip*

- *Pause*

- *Resume my book*

- *Go forward*

- *Go back*

And of course one of the great features of both Audible and Kindle is Whispersync. All your books are synced accross your Amazon account, no matter which device you access them from. Make sure

Whispersync settings are switched on, go to ***Manage Your Content and Devices*** and then ***Settings*** within your main Amazon account - amazon.com/mn/dcw/myx.html

6. AMAZON TAP IN YOUR HOME

News, Weather, and Traffic

When you want a quick peek into the news of the day and current weather, Alexa is standing by with your Flash Briefing. We typically access our briefing while eating breakfast or having our morning coffee.

To set up your personal briefing:

- Choose **Settings > Flash Briefing** on the Alexa App.

- Scroll down the list to toggle on or off news sources such as BBC, ESPN, TMZ and The Economist

- Scroll down to the News Headlines section to select from a variety of categories including Top News, U.S., World, Business, Sports and Offbeat.

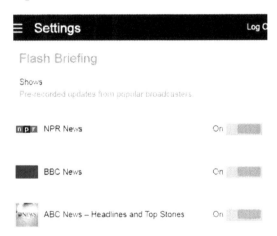

Request this feature with, "**Flash Briefing**" or "**What's in the news?**" The briefing may be short or long, depending on how you customize it.

Request this feature by tapping the microphone button and asking for, "*Flash Briefing*" or "*What's in the news?*" The briefing may be short or long, depending on how you customize it.

When you're being briefed and want to skip to the next source or news story, tap the microphone button and say, "*Next*". You can also ask Alexa to pause the briefing or to repeat the previous story.

If the Weather toggle is on, your briefing will end with current weather conditions for the zip code you provided in the Settings for the Tap device location.

The Amazon Tap arrived set to NPR for the news and the local weather option turned on. Additional weather information can be accessed by asking these questions or queries similar to them.

- *What's the weather for this weekend?"*

- *What's the weather for Tuesday?"*

- *What's the extended forecast?"*

- *What's the weather for next week?"*

- *What's the weather in Chicago?"*

- *Will it rain tomorrow?"*

- *Will it rain in Los Angeles tomorrow?"*

When asked for an extended forecast or the week's weather, the Amazon Tap will provide seven days of weather forecast information.

For traffic information, first go to the Traffic tab in the Alexa app settings. There, you can enter the address of the starting and ending points of your daily commute or a trip you're planning. Additional stops in between can be added and deleted using the buttons.

When you've added these details, ask a question similar to one of these:

- *How is traffic?*

- *What's my commute?*

- *What's traffic like?*

Traffic information is provided by HERE, a company owned by Nokia. The Tap gives you the best route to take given current conditions including volume of traffic and construction. The expected time of your commute is given too.

Movie Showtimes

Gone is the hassle of manually looking up showtimes online or calling the cinema. Instead, simply ask Alexa to relay information on movies showing in your town or the city you'll be heading to on a weekend getaway!

Alexa gets her movie and theater information from IMDB. Here's what you need to do once to setup the Tap:

- Access the Alexa App

- In the Navigation Panel, select *Settings*

- Choose your device (for example, "Jenna's Tap")

- In the Device Location section, choose *Edit*

- Enter your complete address from street name to Zip code

- Choose *Save*

- If your location changes, select *Edit* to change your address

The beauty of it is that you can tailor your search with questions. Here are examples of what you can do:

- Find a specific movie time: Ask, "**When is Zootopia playing?**" or "**When is the movie The Brothers Grimsby playing tomorrow?**"

- Find all your options: Ask, "**What movies are playing?**"

- Find your options for a certain time: Ask, "**What movies are playing between 8pm and 10pm?**"

- Find your options in another city: Ask, "**What movies are playing in Boston?**"

- Find movies in a specific genre: Ask, "**What comedy movies are playing?**"

- Find information about a specific movie: Ask, "**Tell me about the movie Whiskey Tango Foxtrot**."

It is just that easy!

Timers and Alarms

The Amazon Tap has become our go-to choice for setting a timer for baking, knowing when tile grout is ready to use and many other diverse purposes. To set the timer manually, choose **Timer** on the Amazon Alexa app, and set hours, minutes and even seconds, if you really need precision. The maximum is 24 hours. Choose **Start** to begin the countdown.

We typically use voice command for the Timer. It's as easy as tapping the microphone button and saying, "**Set the timer for 45 minutes**". The timer will count down on the app, so a quick glance lets you know how much time is left. You can also ask, "**How much time is left on the timer?**"

A series of pleasant tones sounds when time is up. The timer can be cancelled verbally with something like, "*Cancel timer*". However, the app must be used to pause or resume the timer.

We're pleased to say that Alexa has been upgraded, since its launch, so that you can now set multiple timers or alarms. So to set two timers just tap the microphone button and say "*Set timer for 5 minutes*" and when Alexa confirms the request you can then say "*Set timer for 10 minutes*" and Alexa will set a second timer.

Alarms are equally useful, and the function can be set via the Alarm tab within Timers & Alarms on the app or with a voice command like, "*Set an alarm for 6:45 a.m*". The first few times we set an alarm with the Alexa app, we forgot to toggle it On.

Keep in mind that both setting it and turning it on, just like a conventional alarm clock, are necessary when using the app. When you set an alarm using the voice recognition software, it is automatically turned on.

When the alarm goes off in its gentle tones, cancel it via voice or the app or say, "*Snooze*" to get nine more minutes of rest. Note that you can now set repeating alarms if you need an alarm at the same time each day. Just tap the microphone button and say something like "*Set a repeating alarm for 7am on Monday*"

The timer and alarm volume is set independently in the app. Select **Settings** and your Tap. Scroll to Sounds and adjust it by pressing and dragging the volume bar.

Skills

Alexa boasts a growing menu of voice-driven, real-time skills that greatly add to the Tap's functionality and fun. It's a good bet that these skills, introduced rather late in the evolution of Alexa, will become the features that drive sales going forward.

Alexa skills provide a wealth of information about events, news, restaurants, movies and much more. There are games to entertain you and/or the kids, pithy quotes, an Alexa-led workout, a Skill for ordering event tickets and answers to the whereabouts of your car when someone else is driving it and how much gas it has. Any attempt to adequately summarize the Skills options will fall short, since this list is just the tip of the iceberg.

The majority of Skills are NOT being produced by Amazon. They're developed by the third parties (Domino's Pizza, Warner Brothers, Uber, Yelp, NBC News, Huffington Post, Capital One, to name just a few) to allow them to tap into the growing cadre of Tap users. In fact, with the Alexa Skills Kit (ASK), anyone including you can build a Skill and offer it to the masses! This is the major reason for the rapid growth of Skills.

ASK - http://www.lyntons.com/skills

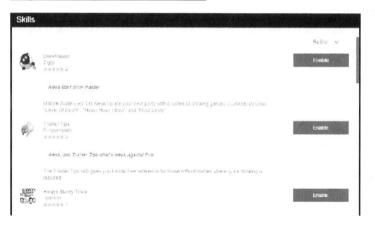

Are you ready to give Skills a try?

- Access the Alexa App

- Choose *Skills* in the Navigation Panel

- Browse the long list of Skills, and read the User Reviews of each, if you would find that helpful

- Enable any Skill you want to explore / Disable them, if desired, using the toggle

- After choosing to Enable the Skill, say something like, "***Turn on [Skill name]*** which will work in most cases, but if it doesn't, click on the Skill to learn more about setup

- Rate the Skill if you'd like, to let others know what you think of it. Choose Write a Review on the Skill detail page, to share your experience

Using Alexa Skills is a growing part of our experience, and we think you'll find them just as useful.

Just to give you a taste of what we're talking about here are two skills that are getting a fair bit of press(remember you need to enable these skills from within the Skills section of the Alexa app before you can use them):

Uber: There's no easier way to get a ride than this! Alexa will order you an Uber car at your request. Here are the quick steps getting started and ordering a ride:

1. Link your Uber account to Alexa

2. Add the location of your Tap in the Alexa app:

- Go to ***Settings***

- Choose the device by name, for example, Ellyn's Tap

- Find the Device Location section, and add the address

3. Try saying:

- ***Ask Uber to send a ride***

- ***Ask Uber to request a car***

- ***Ask Uber to request an UberXL***

4. Ask for the Uber ride status or cancel the Uber

Your Uber Services options include UberX, UberBlack, UberSUV, UberXL and UberSelect.

Domino's Pizza: Ordering a pizza and more for pickup or delivery from Domino's is just as easy as calling for an Uber. You can tract your order too with Domino's Tracker.

Use these quick steps to get ready, set order!

1. Set up a Domino's Pizza Profile at www.Dominos.com if you don't have one

2. You'll need a Domino's Easy Order or recent order saved within your Pizza Profile, so you might have to order online once before being able to use Alexa

3. Try saying:

- *Open Domino's*

- *Open Domino's and place my recent order*

- *Domino's, place my Easy Order*

- *Ask Domino's to track my order* [once it has been placed]

4. Type the phone number saved in your Domino's Pizza Profile into the Alexa app, for an alternate way to get tracking

To-Do and Shopping Lists

Like us, you might soon find these Amazon Tap features indispensable. They are certainly easy to use with either voice commands or the app. Both your Shopping List and To-do List are featured on the main page of the app. Choose the one you want to manually add items or activities to.

For the To-do list, use the *Add Item* box on the app to populate the list. When you complete a task, select the box next to it, and a check mark will appear and the task will be lined through. Finished tasks are moved to the Completed list while the rest remain on the Active list.

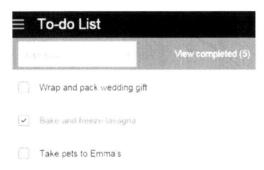

Move back and forth between these lists with the tab at the top of the page. Print the list using the tab at the top. The printer dialog box will appear for you to use to complete the process.

The Alexa personal assistant does a pretty good job populating the list via voice commands, though it might get a word wrong here or there. We asked, "***Add 'find CDs' to my to-do list***", and what appeared on the list was, "***Find c.d.s***". Then, a note to get "screen grabs" was listed as "screen grahams." Misunderstandings happen most often with uncommon words, and we doubt Voice Training would help.

There have been occasions where we've had to cast our minds back and remember what it was we asked Alexa to add because what's on the list doesn't make sense. It's inspired a blend of comedy, frustration and "ah-ha!" moments when we figure it out.

Typically, a request such as, "***Add mow the grass to the to-do list***" is clearly understood. Amazon suggests as an alternate saying something like, "***I need to organize my tools.***"

We've found that the Tap doesn't comprehend this voice command very well. We stick to the "***Add to to-do list***" commands for best results.

Note that checking completed tasks or deleting tasks cannot be done with voice commands; the app must be used. However, you can ask the device something like "***What is on my to-do list***" or "***Read me my to-do list***", and your request will be granted.

Using the Shopping list function is very similar to creating and managing a to-do list:

- Create it with voice commands or manually using the app

- Ask the Tap to read the list to you for review

- Check off items you've purchased, and they are placed on the Completed list which can be viewed with the tab at the page's top

- Delete an item you no longer want

- Print the list using the tab at the top

- Items must be manually removed; voice recognition won't work for this function

The app gives you several choices if you select the down arrow for each item. These include Search Amazon to shop for the item in a new window on Amazon.com or Search Bing to learn more about it or find other buying choices.

Sports

For sports information from your personal assistant, you've got two options. We've discussed one already; choose ESPN and/or Sports headlines as part of your Flash Briefing. The second is to get information by asking the Tap specific questions such as:

- ***What is the score of the Dallas Cowboys game?"***

- ***How are the Boston Red Sox doing?"***

- ***Who won the Kentucky Wildcats game?"***

- *When does the Atlanta Dream play next?"*

- *What time do the Los Angeles Dodgers play tomorrow?"*

At this writing, the Amazon Tap offers scores from the NFL, NBA, WNBA, MLB, MLS, NHL, PGA and NCAA Men's Basketball - www. lyntons.com/scores

If an answer isn't found, the Tap usually includes a link to Bing in the Card it prepares for the query.

The Amazon Tap is able to access a hit-and-miss blend of other sports information. Questions it could answer when we experimented where:

- *Who won the British Open?*

- *Who won the Belmont Stakes?*

We got, "*Sorry, I didn't understand the question I heard*" when asking:

- *Who won the NASCAR race?*

- *Who won the Toledo Mudhens game?*

So, you'll have to ask Alexa if she's a fan of your favorite obscure sport or team!

General Knowledge

The Amazon Tap connects to the Cloud and its vast storehouse of data for measurements, conversions, capital cities, times around the world, mountain heights, population numbers, spelling and pronunciation, etc. Ask a question in these categories, and more than likely, you will receive an accurate answer.

The Tap is excellent with trivia too. For simple answers, ask Alexa about people, dates, stars of movies or their dates of release, Academy Award winners by year and category, singers, lyricists, song and album release dates, World Series and Super Bowl winners and much more. Our guess is that you'll enjoy picking Alexa's brain to discover her fountain of interesting factoids about your favorite topics.

So, ask, "*Who starred in 'To Kill a Mockingbird'?*" and you'll get a list starting with Gregory Peck.

When you want a longer answer, for example, about Gregory Peck, say, "*Wikipedia, Gregory Peck*". The device will read the first paragraph of the Wikipedia entry and also leave a link to the entry in the Card prepared for the query. The Card will also give you the option of searching Bing for the subject.

While the Tap doesn't access recipes, it will provide a link in the prepared Card to a Bing search for recipes for pumpkin bread or whatever it is your mouth is watering for.

In the category of education, this device will be of help with spelling, definitions, conversions, simple calculations, geography, nutritional information and much more that you'll enjoy discovering.

Simon Says?

We've had a few laughs playing Simon Says with Alexa, especially when the kids got in on the act. She'll say most words, phrases and sentences except for recognized curse words. Some marginal words will get repeated. Have some fun with things like, "*Simon says Peter Piper picked a peck of pickled peppers*", and then take it where your imagination leads!

Control Your Home

If you use smart home technology or plan to install some soon, then you'll be excited to know that your Amazon Tap will help you maximize its convenience and benefits. Devices such as WeMo switches, Philips Hue lights and GE wireless lights are among the most popular supported by Amazon Tap, but new and exciting wireless devices are constantly becoming available.

Before you can use your Tap with compatible smart home devices you will need to have gone through the initial set up of these devices in your home.

Products vary from brand to brand but basically in order to get them working you will need to go through a process that involves downloading the manufactures companion app to one of your mobile devices and then setting up the device in your home using that app.

So for example if you are planning to buy and use Philips Hue lights you will need to download the Philips Hue app from either the Amazon app store - www.amazon.com/dp/B00CFDT0C4 - Apple Store - www.lyntons.com/hue-apple - or Google Play store - www.lyntons.com/hue-google - to whichever device you plan to control the lights from and then set up the lights via the app. Some devices like Philips Hue and Wemo just require that they are set up on the same wi-fi network as your Tap. Once they're active you can go to **Settings > Smart Home**. and click "**Discover devices**" and they should show up.

Alexa is looking for devices.

Device discovery can take up to 20 seconds. If you have a Philips Hue bridge, please press the button located on the bridge and then add your devices again.

If you're using a hub service such as Wink Hub to control your connected devices (the option we prefer), you, again need to set up your hub and all devices first and then go to **Settings > Connected Home**. There you can click on "**Link with Wink**" under **Device**

Links. A link will open in your browser where you can log in to your Wink account, which will in turn give your Tap access to the devices controlled by your hub. So as mentioned, go ahead and click "*Discover devices*" within the Alexa app and Alexa will start searching and let you know when she has discovered them all.

Once the search is complete each device will be listed within your app. There within *Settings > Smart Home* in the app you can easily create groups of devices to be controlled with a single command. Click create group and follow the instructions, for example if you have two lights in the bedroom create a group and call it Bedroom Lights, then click on the two devices you want in that group. Once the group is created you can operate those lights with a quick "*Turn on Bedroom Lights*".

You can of course control individual devices with commands like "*Turn on [device name]*"

At the bottom of this Settings page, you'll find the option to *Forget all Smart Home Settings* if you want to remove them from the Tap.

Shopping

For now, your lone shopping option is to re-order products from Amazon that are Prime eligible. For example, we recently ordered wool socks before traveling to the Black Hills of South Dakota to hike.

Alexa was given the command to "Order socks". The device located the previous order and confirmed the brand name and number of pairs in the package. It then asked us, "Should I order it?" A "Yes" was given, and the order was placed.

There are a few things to do on the Echo App to manage your purchases. Go to *Settings > Voice Purchasing*. The Tap comes with the *Purchase by Voice* option in the ON position. It can be toggled to OFF, if you prefer.

Next, if you're concerned about unauthorized purchasing, you have the option of requiring a confirmation code. In the app, type in any 4-digit code you want. The next time you place an order, Alexa will say, for example, "**tell me Jenna's voice code**," which must be given prior to confirming that you want the order to be placed.

Finally, from the app, there's a link to your 1-click payment methods on Amazon.com where you can add, delete or edit credit or debit card information, make address changes and manage related details.

Amazon Echo & Google Calendar

Keeping track of our schedules on a calendar in the cloud gives us the chance to check it from anywhere and to find out what each other has going on. We've used Google Calendar for more than a year and highly recommend it.

It offers calendar views for Day, Week, Month and 4 days. You can also create an Agenda that automatically shows holidays and the birthdays of people you're connected to on Google Plus. Items from the Agenda can be copied to your calendar with notes.

Setting up Your Google Calendar Account

Sign into an existing Google account by selecting your profile picture (it will be generic blue if you haven't added one) on any of the Google pages you use (Search, Gmail, Google+, etc.).

Create a new account on any Google page. You'll either find a Sign Up tab or a Sign In tab that will take you to a page where you can create an account. It takes a minute or so. Through your one Google account, you will be able to set up and use any Google service.

Here's how to begin using Google Calendar once you have a Google account:

- Select **My Account**

- Locate Google Calendar among your options, and choose it

- On Amazon Tap, open the Amazon Echo App

- Choose **Settings > Calendar**

- Click "Link the Google Calendar account"

www.google.com/calendar

When we first tried it, we got an error message that opened in a new window. We simply closed the window and tried again, and got a window with a message that "Alexa would like to: View your email address, View your basic profile info and Manage your calendars".

Select the circled "i" next to each topic for more information, or simple choose "Accept". This step failed the first time too, but succeeded on the second attempt.

Accessing Your Google Calendar With the Echo App

For now, you can't add items to your calendar directly from the Alexa app, manually or by voice, without a work-around which we describe shortly.

You'll have to add items to the Calendar while on Google. Once you've done so, you can ask Alexa what's on your calendar. You'll be given the next four events within the next month. Also for now, calendars that others share with you and holiday calendars are not supported.

Okay, about that work-around we mentioned: There is a way to add events to your Google Calendar using the Tap, and we discuss it fully in our **chapter on IFTTT**.

Those letters stand for "**If This, Then That**" and represent a way to use one device, the Tap in this case, to trigger something to happen on another device or app.

Take a look at the IFTTT chapter for the "recipe" for "Add Amazon Tap to-do item to Google Calendar." There, you'll discover how to use the Tap for sending Quick Add Event reminders to the Google Calendar.

Add an Adult to Your Tap Household

When Alexa joins the family, don't be surprised if your significant other wants to be BFF's with her! Each Amazon Tap Household account supports up to two adults.

Our favorite perk of being on the Household account together is that we are able to share our music and content libraries with one another. For example, at the top of the Amazon Prime Homepage on the Alexa app, the top tab allows us to toggle between our two Libraries. At this writing, Amazon Tap cannot access children's content that may be part of your Amazon Household account.

Additionally, we can both use Voice Purchasing which is discussed in the Shopping section of this guide. Voice Purchasing can be set up under **Settings > Voice Purchasing** where you'll select your options.

To add a household member, go to the **Settings** and select **Household Profile**. A new tab on your browser will open where you'll sign into your Amazon account and be taken to a page with the heading "Invite a household member." The page includes a brief description of the benefits.

When you continue, the screen will ask you to pass the device you're using to the person you're inviting to join the Household account. They'll sign into their Amazon account.

In a minute or two the second user's music and content libraries will be available for sharing. To leave the Tap Household or remove a member, go to S**ettings > In an Amazon household with...** There, select your choice.

As a precaution, a popup window appears asking you to confirm or cancel your selection.

Voice Commands and Things to Try

We hope that we have helped you find your way around your Amazon Tap and you now have a good working knowledge of the features available and how to use voice commands. Our aim has been to go beyond a dry repetition of the basic functions and share with you how we actually use the Tap in our daily lives.

We of course appreciate that you will probably have your own preferences so before we move on we would like to draw your attention to a very useful reference.

There is a full and extensive list of voice commands that you can find in Amazon's help pages online.

This information is repeated within the Alexa app, just scroll down the left column and click on *"**Things to Try**"*. As well as voice commands you can also keep up to date with new features.

7. THE TAP AND IFTHISTHENTHAT (IFTTT)

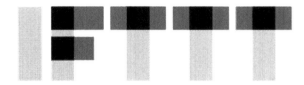

Have you ever lost your phone and asked someone to call it, so you could hear it ring and locate it? Now with the help of something called IFTTT, your Tap can be used for dozens of tasks just like this that it cannot accomplish by itself.

IFTTT is a third-party service supported by the Amazon Tap. It creates rules, called recipes, which allow your devices to work with other apps and websites to accomplish tasks. Triggering a call to your phone by, for example, asking Alexa what's on your to-do list is just one of many ways you can expand the functionality of your Amazon Tap with IFTTT.

The service sounded like little more than a novelty to us when we first explored it, we must admit. However, we were soon enthusiastic about the connection between the Tap and IFTTT and use it on a regular basis, if not yet daily.

The letters IFTTT stand for IF This Then That. Let's explain using the example we've mentioned:

IF This: You ask *"Alexa, what's on my to-do list?"*

Then That: Alexa places a call to your cell phone.

Combinations like this one are called **If Recipes**, If I do This, Then That will happen. Quite a few of them work with Alexa. The "If" side of the equation is known as the Trigger; it is the event that causes the action to occur.

The fact that a trigger such as asking Alexa to review your to-do list seemingly has nothing to do with a phone call being made shouldn't confuse you. You're simply asking the Amazon Tap to do something it knows how to do and then connecting technology to that function that will cause something unrelated to occur.

IFTTT also offers Do Recipes for smart phones and tablets in combination with an app for each task. Turning on and off Philips hue lighting, setting your Nest thermostat and saving receipts to Evernote are just three of hundreds of tasks you can accomplish with Do Recipes.

However, currently, Do Recipes do not work with the Tap. In addition, the Tap cannot be the recipient of an action, just the trigger, or the "if" part of an If Recipe.

While Do Recipes aren't pertinent to our discussion of the Tap, we recommend you check them out. There are some awesome recipes available that will add convenience and productivity to your life in the same way the If Recipes do.

Still confused? Read on...

Start by Activating the Amazon Alexa Channel on IFTTT - Getting started took us about three minutes. Here's how to do it:

- Go to the Amazon Alexa Channel on IFTTT - www.lyntons. com/alexa - and Sign In to an existing account or Sign Up for your first account

- Sign in

- Select **Connect**

- Sign into your Amazon account in the pop-up window

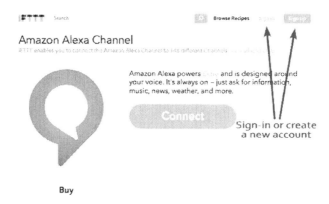

Using Your Tap With IFTTT

Once we were signed in and set up we set aside a half hour or so to familiarize ourselves with the If Recipes - www.lyntons.com/if - that can be accomplished by creating relationships between the Tap, apps and other devices.

A few hours later, we were still having fun exploring and trying many of the recipes. At this writing, there are about 250 If Recipes on the IFTTT Alexa page, and more are being written regularly.

Here's a tip: Explore the IFTTT site using your Android or iOS mobile tablet or phone rather than a PC or MAC. You'll likely want to use some of the If Recipes, and to do so, you'll find that some of them require you to download the other necessary 3rd party apps to your phone or tablet. It is these 3rd party apps that actually implement the action that is triggered when you give a specific order to Alexa.

Top If Recipes for Alexa

Our "top" recipes might not be yours once you've had a chance to explore the possibilities, but we have found these to be very handy. You'll see that each one of these has an "if" task that will create a "then" result.

Ask Alexa to locate your phone: (www.lyntons.com/findphone) Let's see how the example from above works in practice. Even if you don't activate this recipe now, it's a great one to keep in mind for that inevitable time when the phone goes missing in the couch, car or coffee shop.

- **If:** You ask Alexa, *"Alexa, what's on my to-do list?"*

- **Then:** Alexa will call your phone

How: To set up this recipe click the Connect tab to connect to the Phone Call Channel. A new window opens, send your phone number to the Phone Call Channel and you'll receive a phone call with an activation PIN. Enter the PIN and you're done. Now when you say the trigger *"Alexa, what's on my to-do list?"* your phone will receive a call.

Find My Phone: (www.lyntons.com/find) is a similar related recipe that turns up your android phone's volume to make it easier to hear and locate when it is called.

Email yourself your shopping list via Tap: (www.lyntons.com/list) Take your shopping list to the store with you on your phone.

- **If:** You ask, *"Alexa, what's on my shopping list?"*

- **Then:** The Tap will email you the entire list.

How: First, add your email address to the box on the ITFFF recipe page. Then, make your request of Alexa, and the email of your shopping list will show up in your inbox shortly.

If you already use OneNote, send your shopping list there in short order with this recipe - www.lyntons.com/note.

You can email yourself your to-do list just as easily - www.lyntons.com/todo.

Or, transfer your to-do list - www.lyntons.com/evernote - or your shopping list - www.lyntons.com/evernote1 - from the Alexa App to Evernote.

In addition to sending a short email or emailing yourself your to-do or shopping list, there are other email-related If Recipes you might find helpful:

- Accomplish something from your to-do list and send a clapping gif - www.lyntons.com/clap - to friends or family. Yes, okay a bit silly but surprisingly satisfying.

- Send yourself the new items you've added to your to-do list - www.lyntons.com/newtodo

- Send your to-do list to a Wunderlist account - www.lyntons.com/wunder - or to OmniFocus - www.lyntons.com/omni

- Most of the recipes involving email allow you to include up to five email addresses.

Add Amazon Tap to-do item to Google Calendar: (www.lyntons.com/calendar) This recipe publishes "quick add event" items to your Google Calendar when you add it to your to-do list.

- **If:** You ask, "*Alexa, add appointment with Ellen at 1pm to my to-do list.*"

- **Then:** The appointment will be added to the Google Calendar at the point on the calendar the request was made. In other words, if I make the request of Alexa at 9:23am, that is where it will appear on my Google Calendar, to serve as a reminder. I can leave it there, or type it into the 1pm slot when I'm reviewing the calendar. If this sounds complicated, it won't be once you do it and see how it works.

How: On the recipe page, simply select "*Add*," and the connection between Amazon Tap and Google Calendar will be made. This assumes of course that you have already linked your Google calendar to your Amazon Tap.

Print your shopping list with an HP wireless printer: (www. lyntons.com/print) Use voice to create a list and a simple command to have the list printed. Oh course you will need an HP wireless printer and an HP Connected Account.

- **If:** You ask, "Alexa, what's on my shopping list?"

- **Then:** Your list will print.

How: The Tap will send the list to the printer when you connect via the recipe page.

Turn on the lights when you play music: (www.lyntons.com/ lights) This If Recipe works with Philips hue lighting that you've added to your *Settings > Smart Home > Devices.*

- **If:** You play music from your Music Library, Prime Music, Tunein or iHeartRadio.

- **Then**: Your Philips hue lighting will turn on.

How: Simply connect via the Philips hue Channel on the recipe page where you will log into your Philips account.

Philips Wi-Fi lighting is hugely popular with smart home enthusiasts, and the number of If Recipes that make use of Philips hue bears that out. Here are a few of the many other recipes to try with Philips hue lights:

- Ask Alexa to change the light color (www.lyntons.com/ colorswap)

- Ask Alexa to toggle all hue lights on or off (www.lyntons.com/ togglehue)

- Change light color when a set timer goes off (www.lyntons. com/timer)

- Change hue light color each time a new song plays (www. lyntons.com/songchange)

- Blink hue lights when a set timer goes off (www.lyntons.com/ blink-hue)

- Blink my lights when I check off an item on my to-do list (www. lyntons.com/blink-todo)

Turn on a WeMo switch when an alarm goes off: (www. lyntons.com/wemo) WeMo switches are Wi-Fi connected switches. They are plugged into standard outlets. Then, a lamp can be plugged into the WeMo and turned on. From there, the WeMo switch can be toggled on or off with a Wi-Fi device and app.

- **If:** An Alexa App alarm goes off.

- **Then:** The WeMo switch will turn on.

How: Add the WeMo switch to your Alexa app at *Settings>Smart Home>Devices*. Manually turn the switch on. On the recipe page, connect to the WeMo Switch channel. Then, set an Tap alarm for when you want that switch to be energized.

Set the thermostat temperature: (www.lyntons.com/temp-nest) This recipe is for the Nest wireless thermostat, but a recipe is available for the popular Ecobee thermostat (www.lyntons.com/ temp-ecob) too.

- **If:** You add an item to your to-do list.

- **Then:** The recipe will allow you to set the thermostat to the desired temperature.

How: On the recipe page, connect to the Nest Thermostat Channel, and follow directions from there.

You've Got Options

As you browse the recipes, you'll find more than one for some of the same tasks. This simply means that the recipes were created by different users. In our experience, any two recipes that do the same thing work equally well, but we haven't tried them all. You might have to experiment with a couple of If Recipes to find the one that works best for you.

The My Recipes Page

Once you use an If Recipe, it will be added to your My Recipes Page (www.lyntons.com/my-recipes) to access again later. Simply select any recipe from that page to use it as you created it. You can also use the Edit button, discussed below, to tweak it for each use.

Next to each recipe are your options. Hover over each one to see its function. The buttons are:

- **The On/Off Button:** This allows you to turn the recipe off when you don't want it to respond to trigger input and back on again when you do. For example, we keep the recipe "Find your phone by asking '*Alexa, what's on my to-do list*'" off. It's ready to switch on should we misplace the phone, which happens more than we care to admit!

- **The Reload/Check Recipe Now Button:** Selecting this button checks for trigger data immediately. At this writing, IFTTT checks for triggers every 15 minutes for most recipes. If you want to trigger the recipe immediately, select this button.

- **The View Recipe Log Button:** This is a list of actions taken for this recipe and when they occurred. The list includes the creation of the recipe, each time it was triggered and when it was turned on or off. The list shows your last 100 actions for that recipe.

- **The Edit Button:** Selecting this button takes you to an edit page where you can turn the recipe on or off, check it, view the log and delete the recipe from your My Recipes list. You can also publish recipes you've created. For creating recipes, see below. On the Edit page, you can also change the email recipient or add recipients, change the text on the subject line of the email that goes out and include a URL as an attachment to the email. If this sounds confusing, it will become clear with just a little experience managing recipes, as it did for us.

Note: When you've made edits to any recipe, be sure to select the *Update* button to put them into effect.

Create Your Own Recipes

Now, if you've been paying attention you will have noticed that many of the recipes have the same triggers, for example many of the recipes are activated when you say "Alexa, what's on my to-do list". The reason for this is that currently there are only a limited amount of trigger commands available; although we suspect this will change in the future. So what do you do if there are two recipes you want to use but they both have the same trigger command, after all you don't want to say one command and have two actions happening at the same time? The answer is to create your own new recipe. Near the top of the *My Recipes* page, you'll notice the **Create a Recipe** button.

Select it to be taken to an intermediate page with a big "ifthisthanthat".

It seems this page is redundant and could be skipped, with users being taken directly to the first step of creating your recipe. We suspect it might be removed at some point, perhaps before you are reading this, so if you don't see that page you'll know why! On the intermediate page, select the blue-lettered "this" to be taken to the first step of the recipe-building process

The steps are simple to follow, but here's an overview:

- **Step 1: Choose Trigger Channel**

  For the Tap, IFTTT calls the trigger channel **Amazon Alexa**. It's the only trigger that works with the Tap. If you're creating recipes for other devices, you'll find channels for Android and iOS devices and dozens of apps for services, retailers and more.

- **Step 2: Choose a Trigger**

  Here, you will select the specific "If This" action you want as the trigger. Options include asking Alexa a question such as what's on your to-do or shopping list, adding an item to either of those lists or a Tap timer you have set going off.

  As mentioned you can now set your own trigger phrase which is definitely the best thing to do. So click the option that says

"Say a specific phrase" and you will be taken to a box where you can input, in lower case, the phase you would like to use. The phrase will begin "*Alexa, Trigger...*" so it is the rest of the phrase that you need to enter in the box. So for example if you have set up a Nest Thermostat in your home and linked it to your Alexa App you could create the trigger "Trigger nest to 65" in which case you would enter "nest to 65" in the box.

- **Step 3: Create the Trigger**

  Select the "*Create Trigger*" button, and you've completed the "If This" half of the recipe. Once you select the button, a screen showing "If [Tap symbol] then that" appears with the "that" in blue for you to select.

  Its purpose is to show you that you've completed the "If This" steps, but in our opinion, seems to be another useless step. If you don't see it when you create your first recipe, you'll know it has been removed to streamline the process.

- **Step 4: Choose an Action Channel**

  Here, you select the device or app that you want to carry out the "Then That" action such as send an email, set a thermostat, make a phone call, load a photo to Facebook or Pinterest, adjust lighting or turn on an appliance. In our example above you would search out and click the Nest Thermostat action channel.

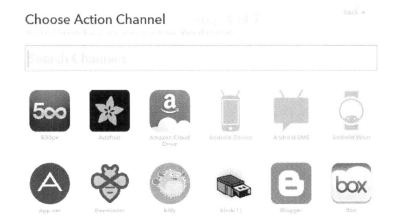

- **Step 5: Choose an Action**

  You've selected a "channel" to carry out the "Then That" action, now specify just what you want to happen. For example, if you've selected your Philips hue lighting, you can turn it on or off, cause it to blink or change colors or perform any of its other capabilities. Or in the example above you would have the option to set your Nest thermostat to 65 degrees.

- **Step 6: Complete Action Fields**

  In this step, additional specifics, the "ingredients" of your recipe, are added. For example, if the Channel (Step 4) is Gmail and the Action (Step 5) is to send an email, in Step 6 you'll choose the email's recipient, subject and text. If the Channel is Nest and the Action is to set your thermostat, Step 6 will be to select your preferred temperature and other options such as choosing the heating or cooling function to complete the desired Action.

M Complete Action Fields

Send an email

M To address

M Subject

Score of the   AskedTeamName   Game

- **Step 7: Create and Connect**

  You'll see the details of the recipe in the Recipe Title box. If it is correct, choose the Create Recipe button, and your recipe will be created. You'll be taken to your **My Recipes** page, and the newly created recipe will appear at the top of the list.

We've tried a couple dozen existing recipes and created a handful more. We're still exploring and adding recipes, and we've found that several have become very useful for adding things to our to-do list or calendar, creating reminders and managing parts of our home automation system.

As with any new gadget or app, there's a short learning curve for IFTTT basics and then an ongoing period spent finding, creating and customizing Recipes to give us maximum convenience and functionality. We're enjoying the process, and think that you will too.

9. TROUBLESHOOTING YOUR AMAZON TAP

Our experience with the Amazon Tap has been pleasantly trouble-free, and we expect the same for you. However, some users do experience problems. The vast majority of them are minor and can be easily solved.

Below is a list of issues and the steps you should take to try to resolve them. We reference the Things to Try (www.lyntons.com/try) list several times. That list can be accessed on Amazon, and it is also included in your Alexa App.

The Tap Doesn't Understand You

Try these:

- Eliminate background talking or other noise that could be confusing the voice recognition technology

- Speak clearly and more slowly

- Complete Voice Training with the Tap, so that it improves its ability to understand you. Visit the Alexa app's Voice Training section.

- Phrase your request differently; The list of Things to Try includes topic pages where you'll find requests the Tap understands.

The Tap Can't Give You an Answer

Try these:

- Repeat the question

- Rephrase the question; See the list of Things to Try for help

- State the question more specifically or more broadly

- Let the Tap know you're asking a question by saying, for example, "*Question: What's the capital of Romania?*"

- Keep in mind that the Tap can't answer every question, though its capabilities continue to expand. By exploring the Things to Try list, you'll gain a better understanding of what questions the Amazon Tap can and cannot answer

The Tap Plays the Wrong Music

Try these:

- Check your Cards (your history) on the Alexa App Homepage to see what the app heard you say

- Check to see if the music you requested is in your library or available from Amazon Prime Music

Voice Purchasing Code Doesn't Work

Try these:

- Locate the On/Off toggle on the Alexa App under **Settings > Voice Purchasing** and make sure it is on

- In the same location, **Settings > Voice Purchasing**, make sure that you've chosen a code and are using the right one in your attempt to make a purchase

Tap Won't Connect To Wi-Fi

Try these:

- If not connected, go to the Alexa App Homepage, open the navigation panel on the left, and select *Settings > Set up a new device > Tap*

- Press and hold the *Bluetooth/Wi-Fi* Button for about five seconds, and the light ring will turn orange while your mobile device, if using one with the Tap, connects to it

- Choose your Wi-Fi network from the list that appears, and enter the network password if necessary

- Select *Connect*

- If your network isn't on the list, scroll down to select *Re-scan* to search again or choose *Add a Network* and follow the instructions

- When connection to the Wi-Fi network is completed, a confirmation message will appear in the app

Tap Won't Connect to Bluetooth

Try these:

- Bring your Bluetooth phone or other device within 30 feet of the Amazon Tap

- Turn on the device's Bluetooth connection

- Check the Card on your Alexa App to see if it is hearing, "Connect".

- Alternatively, find the Tap in your device's Bluetooth settings menu, and manually select the Amazon Tap to attempt to connect

- If you're still having trouble, go to **Settings > [Your Tap's name] > Bluetooth**, and select **Remove** to clear all paired devices

- Pair your Tap to your Bluetooth device again

- Hold down the Taps power button for 5 seconds. Then press the button again to turn on the device. Repeat the pairing instructions

Tap Can't Discover a Connected Home Device

Try these basics first:

- Make sure the device is on the list of Supported Home Devices (www.lyntons.com/supported) for Amazon Tap

- Set up the manufacturer's companion app for the device, if you haven't done so

- For Wink and Wink-connected devices, link your Wink account by following the steps at Connect a Hub Service (www.lyntons.com/connect-a-hub) to Amazon Tap

- Use the device's companion app to check to see that it has been properly set up, and if it isn't, refer to the device's guide or website

- Use the devices companion app to download any available updates including fixes to ensure the best connectivity

- Connect your Amazon Tap to the same Wi-Fi network as the device, so Tap can discover it

- To do this, go to the Alexa App and update your Wi-Fi network at **Settings > [Your Tap] > Update Wi-Fi**; we suggest you use your home network since work or school networks might not allow unrecognized devices to connect

- If there is still no connection, say, "***Discover my devices***"

- If the device is a Philips hue bridge, press the button on the bridge and hold it while instructing the Tap to discover your devices

- If the Tap says, "Discovery is complete. I couldn't find any devices," check again to make sure the Tap and the device are connected to the same Wi-Fi network

Note that some devices can only connect to a 2.4GHz Wi-Fi network. These include:

- WeMo Insight Light Switch

- WeMo Insight Switch

- WeMo Switch

- Wink Hub

5 GHz networks: If you're using your Tap on a 5GHz Wi-Fi network, switch to a 2.4GHz network to discover and connect the device. If your router is dual band, and you don't know the name of the 2.4GHz network, check the router settings on your computer or contact the router's manufacturer for help.

Enable SSDP or UPnP on your router: This can be done via the router settings on your computer. If you can't locate them, contact the router manufacturer or its website.

Choose an easy name: If your connected home devices are discovered, but Tap doesn't process the request, perhaps it is because you've assigned a difficult name to the group.

Change it to something simple like **Kitchen Lights** or **Hall Switch**. If the device or group was named via the manufacturer's companion app, that's where the name change must be made.

Restart your Amazon Tap by unplugging it and plugging it back in. Restart your connected home device by following the user guide for it.

Reset your Amazon Tap: Occasionally a seemingly stubborn problem is solved easily by resetting the Amazon Tap. First, simply restart it as described immediately above. If the issue isn't fixed, then reset the Tap using the reset button on the bottom of the unit.

Reset:

- Use paper clip or similar tool to press and hold the reset button for five seconds

- Watch the top light ring as it turns orange and then blue

- When it turns off and then blue again, this indicates it is in setup mode

- Open the Amazon Alexa App to connect your device to a Wi-Fi network and register it to your Amazon account

9. SECURITY

In this era of breaches of financial data and government agencies monitoring private conversations, it's no surprise that Amazon Tap users are concerned about privacy issues. When we read that the Tap processes and stores information in the Cloud, it sounds like a large, nebulous location where it might be difficult to maintain security.

The Cloud isn't a huge pool that anyone can access. Instead, it is a series of large computer systems and servers owned by private and publicly traded companies and located around the world. These systems support the Internet and its millions of sites and billions of devices.

Cloud computing is growing steadily, and you might already do business with companies using the Cloud. These include Apple, Google, Netflix, Flickr, Yahoo Mail and Microsoft. Banks are using the Cloud for storing and processing date and a rate that is increasing. According to recent analysis, the average bank uses more than 800 Cloud services.

The computers and servers that make up the Cloud use the best security available, and there's a reasonable expectation that the information you speak to your Amazon Tap will be secure. Besides, most of us aren't making requests of Alexa to remember our social security number or credit card number. Most requests we make would be of no value to anyone or risk to us should they become known.

Okay, Let's Cover Some Specifics About the Security of Your Amazon Tap Account.

What you say to the Tap is processed and stored in the Cloud: By now, you're probably familiar with the Cards the Amazon Alexa App produces each time you give it a command or ask a question. They're available for review on the app homepage. Each card represents a voice recording that is also stored in the Cloud. Here is more information straight from the Amazon Tap FAQs:

The Tap uses the recordings, especially when you give feedback about whether or not it heard you correctly, to improve its voice recognition abilities. Over time, it is learning to understand you better in order to give you better results.

You can delete the cards, and the voice recordings are deleted too. Here is what Amazon says regarding this practice, again from the FAQs (www.lyntons.com/faqs):

"How do I delete individual voice recordings?"

You can delete specific voice interactions with Amazon Tap by going to **History** in Settings in the Amazon Tap App, drilling down for a specific entry, and then tapping the **Delete** button."

"Can I delete all my voice recordings?

Yes, you can delete the Amazon Tap voice recordings. Doing so will delete related Home Screen cards, and may degrade your experience using Amazon Tap. To delete the recordings associated with your account, visit **Manage Your Content and Devices** at www. amazon.com/myx and select **Amazon Tap**, or contact customer service. While a deletion request is being processed, the Amazon Alexa App may still display and allow you to play back the voice recordings that are being deleted. You can delete specific voice interactions with Amazon Tap by going to **History** in Settings in the Amazon Alexa App, drilling down for a specific entry, and then tapping the **Delete** button."

In conclusion, the information you speak to the Amazon Tap is very likely as safe as your banking and credit card information. If you have any remaining concerns, be selective about what questions and commands you give to the Tap, and delete any you would be uncomfortable about someone else accessing.

10. YOUR FUTURE WITH ALEXA

We expect the practical benefits of using our Tap to go through the roof in the days ahead. Just as an example, when our Tap arrived a few months ago, before we published this book, it didn't support Google Calendar.However, within a month, that changed, and we happily linked our Amazon Tap to Google Calendar. Just recently, support for the Pandora music service was added, and while that wasn't huge for us, a couple of nieces who visit often thought it "way cool." And just before we went to print the Skills section appeared, so clearly there's a lot more to come.

So What Lies Ahead? Let's Make Some Educated Guesses

Amazon will develop and add new services and form more partnerships with third-party providers. This is happening consistently. Since we've fired up our first Echo, ESPN Radio has joined Spotify, Pandora and Google Calendar as new additions.

We expect Amazon to sell an enormous number of Taps, and that will create growing demand for services providing customizable news, music, sports, weather and specialty channels. As partnerships are formed, your Tap will be updated to take advantage of the new options.

IFTTT is hot, and so are the technologies such as home automation and Cloud computing that make many of the recipes possible. In addition, most of us will purchase additional Wi-Fi gadgets in the coming years, part of the burgeoning "Internet of things" (devices connected and controlled online).

These trends and the potential of IFTTT mean that your Amazon Tap will likely become far more useful for important parts of your lifestyle such as:

- Home automation of lighting, HVAC, appliances, home theater, sound system, etc.

- Scheduling and time management

- Shopping

- Social media

- Control of your smart devices

Exciting new apps for the Alexa are on the way. We anticipate this because Amazon has invited a chosen array of tech-savvy developers to try their hand at creating apps in addition to the standard Alexa App that supports its functionality.

The word is that the software development kit the developers are given by Amazon supports Java, JavaScript, Node.js, Python, PHP and Ruby programming languages. This means that all of us can expect diverse and highly functional apps to be developed that will make our experience with the Amazon Tap that much more awesome!

A Final Quick Reminder About Updates

As we mentioned at the start of this book,The Amazon Tap and indeed all media streaming services, like Apple TV, Roku and the Chromecast, are still in their infancy. The landscape is changing all the time with new services, apps and media suppliers appearing daily.

Staying on top of new developments is our job and if you sign up to our free monthly newsletter we will keep you abreast of news, tips and tricks for all your streaming media equipment.

If you want to take advantage of this, sign up for the updates here (www.lyntons.com/updates): Don't worry; we hate spam as much as you do so we will never share your details with anyone.

35078980R00051

Made in the USA
Middletown, DE
18 September 2016